First published in Great Britain in 2000 by
Westzone Publishing Ltd
27 Adam & Eve Mews, London W8 6UG

Text © **Zed Nelson**
Introduction © **Daniel Lazare**

Photographs © **Zed Nelson**

10 9 8 7 6 5 4 3 2 1

A catalogue record for this book is available
from the British Library

ISBN 0 9537438 3 7

Design
Rose Design, London
in collaboration with **Zed Nelson**

Printing and lithography
Salto, Belgium

Gun Nation Zed Nelson

For Tyler, who didn't let it stop him...

Foreword
Zed Nelson

IT WAS ON ASSIGNMENT IN AFGHANISTAN WHEN IT ALL WENT TERRIBLY WRONG.

Travelling in a small blue saloon car through the war-ravaged capital, Kabul, we were in the wrong place at a bad time. The first bullet shattered the windscreen. There was little glamour in what followed. My friend and working colleague, Tyler, was shot horribly in both arms. One high-velocity bullet tore through his upper arm, severing nerves and tissue, while another exploded the bone in his forearm, leaving a limp and shattered limb, pulsing blood. Our guide and interpreter, Sabur,was shot through the neck. The bullet entered cleanly and would have exited the other side if it hadn't hit his jawbone. Eighteen bullets punched through the car as if it was made of tinfoil. What took place inside that velour-upholstered Toyota was something that isn't supposed to happen. It was nothing like the movies.

GUNS SEEM TO HAVE FOLLOWED ME AROUND MOST OF MY WORKING LIFE.

In Somalia in 1992, I watched a nation tear itself apart with weapons donated by the United States and Russia. Deadly gifts of the Cold War. In Angola the story was much the same, only their guns came from other sources too. In El Salvador, the freedom fighters were using hand-me-down M-16's originally supplied to the Nicaraguan Contras – who gratefully received consignments of assault rifles from the United States to help them kill the Commies of the day. And finally, in Afghanistan, as Mujahideen guerrilla fighters battled an occupying Russian army, the US helped tip the balance once again. With more guns.

Who knows if the weapons that abruptly ended our Afghan adventure were Russian or American? It hardly matters. The other men I saw die that day had stepped into a minefield, and those landmines could have been British or Chinese. Few come out of the politics of war with a clear conscience.

For me, it was time to focus closer to home, to shine that revealing spotlight into our own back yard. Mayhem and suffering are easier to stomach with an exotic, foreign flavour: Africa, the Middle East, Eastern Europe. As long as they're black, Muslim or former Communists. Save the colour film for celebrity profiles and hometown lifestyle features.

THE FINAL CATALYST FOR GUN NATION WAS SOMETHING THAT HAPPENED IN BRITAIN.

Something grotesque and new. A man in a junior school with a gun. Sixteen children and their teacher shot to death, with a legally-owned firearm. The Dunblane Massacre.

While politicians and lobbyists argued over gun laws in Britain, I arrived in America – a country that has historically embraced and celebrated gun ownership.

MOST AMERICAN GUN OWNERS CONSIDER THEMSELVES NORMAL, LAW-ABIDING CITIZENS.

40% of US households reportedly keep at least one gun.

At the National Rifle Association's 125th annual convention in Dallas, I first heard the mantra of the staunchly pro-gun advocates: "Guns don't kill people – people kill people", always followed closely by, "A gun is an inanimate object".

Those words followed me everywhere. In the first year of my travels in America, over 34,000 people were shot to death with inanimate objects.

A WELL REGULATED MILITIA, BEING NECESSARY TO THE SECURITY OF A FREE STATE, THE RIGHT OF THE PEOPLE TO KEEP AND BEAR ARMS, SHALL NOT BE INFRINGED.

Second Amendment to the US Constitution, adopted 1791

Introduction
Daniel Lazare

As they got ready to go to class at Columbine High School on the morning of April 20, 1999, Dylan Klebold and Eric Harris carefully concealed an assault weapon, a short-barrelled rifle, and a pair of sawn-off shotguns beneath their coats. These were weapons that a friend had purchased on their behalf at one of Colorado's many unregulated 'gun shows' – travelling free markets in which private weapons dealers ask no names, require no signatures, and call nobody for a background check. When Klebold and Harris then used the guns to kill twelve classmates, a teacher, and finally themselves, the result was a frenzied national debate about America's runaway gun culture and where it was heading. Shocked parents denounced the National Rifle Association and demanded that something be done, pollsters reported a dramatic surge in public support for stricter controls, and television commentators solemnly announced that America had finally turned a corner.

And then – nothing. A proposal to close the gun-show loophole by imposing a three-day waiting period so that police could run background checks on would-be purchasers died in Congress. So did bills to ban the importation of large-capacity ammunition clips and to require trigger locks or other safety devices. Other proposals requiring that gun owners be licensed or that dealers keep detailed records so that investigators could determine who sold what weapon to whom were considered so controversial that they didn't even get off the ground. Not only did the Columbine High School massacre fail to make a dent in the American gun culture, but considering that the National Rifle Association's membership shot up from 2.7 to 3.4 million over the ensuing twelve months, it may very well have succeeded in kicking it up into an even higher gear.

How could this be? What is it about the American love affair with firearms that makes it so resistant to change? Readers should keep in mind as they ponder Zed Nelson's superb photographic account of America's bizarre gun culture, that the proud owners of assault rifles, semi-automatic handguns and other weapons are not fringe elements on the margins of American society. Rather, they are participants in a long-running constitutional conflict – perhaps deadlock is a better word – over the meaning and nature of liberty. This kulturkampf divides America into two warring camps. On one side are millions of citizens who do not own guns themselves, cannot understand those who do, and can't imagine how private weapons stashes can wreak anything but havoc in a modern society. On the other side is a smaller but still significant portion of the population – one adult in three according to opinion polls – which believes that guns are important not only as a means of defence, but as an example of the kind of freedom that liberals, environmentalists, and other unpatriotic sorts are constantly trying to take away. To say that gun owners regard freedom of this sort as valuable would be a vast understatement. Quite simply, many see it as the greatest gift to mankind since Moses came down from the mountaintop with a pair of stone tablets. It is a specifically American legacy that patriots have pledged their lives, fortunes, and sacred honour (to quote the Declaration of Independence) to defend. Since item number two in that legacy is a constitutional amendment seemingly guaranteeing an unlimited right to bear arms, many have pledged to defend that to the death as well.

Thus, guns do not merely symbolise freedom from this point of view. Rather, like the religious icons that the Eastern Orthodox believe contain the actual spirit of God, they are freedom itself. The fact that troubled teenagers, neo-Nazis, and crazed day traders occasionally use them to knock off students, postmen and other innocents is immaterial. Such incidents are the price of liberty. As National Rifle Association president Charlton Heston – who once played Moses in the movies – put it shortly after the Columbine High School massacre: 'In the words of Ben Franklin, "Those who would give up their freedom to purchase a little security… deserve neither freedom nor security."' Freedom is precious in and of itself regardless of the lives lost as a consequence.

Of course, some people might counter that freedom from gun-wielding maniacs is no less valid than freedom to wield a gun oneself. But this runs contrary to a corollary to the above theory of an especially American legacy of freedom, namely that some freedoms are more important than others. Freedoms bequeathed by America's Founding Fathers are the ones that count not just because they are enshrined in the Bill of Rights, but because to think otherwise would mean believing that today's Americans know as much as the Founders did, that they are capable of creating new freedoms to take the place of old ones, and that they are free to move society in whatever direction they may wish. To the contrary, traditionalists contend that America's ancient charter of liberty must be obeyed in toto. Just as the ancient Israelites were free only to obey Yahweh's commandments, Americans today are free only to adhere to the blueprint laid down by their own tribal patriarchs.
If this sounds crazy, it is. The United States is hardly the only society to wrestle with the problem of tradition versus modernity. But it is the only allegedly modern nation to do so in such an extreme fashion, at such a late date, and on such a grand scale. In other industrialised countries, tradition for the most part is embedded in a specific institution – in the church, for instance, the monarchy, or the military. In the United States, it is part and parcel of the entire legal fabric. The Constitution, of which the Bill of Rights is a part, is not simply a law, but the 'law of laws'. It is the source of all legal and political authority, yet at the same time is largely unchangeable. While 'we the people' have modified the original document on seventeen different occasions since the 1790s, rarely have we done so in any fundamental way and never have we tampered with that holy of holies, the Bill of Rights. Given the overwhelming public prejudice against even trying, it would be like trying to repeal the Declaration of Independence or the Gettysburg Address. The result, to quote Thomas Jefferson, is 'like the arc [sic] of the covenant, too sacred to be touched' – a document, in other words, that is all but written in stone.

This means, of course, that everything it contains is written in stone also. If everything in the Bill of Rights was like the First Amendment, the one beginning with the words, 'Congress shall make no law respecting an establishment of religion… or abridging the freedom of speech', this might not be a problem. But the Second Amendment, the one that speaks of a right to bear arms, is a horse of a different colour. For years, liberals thought they had solved the problem of the troublesome Second through the miracle of re-interpretation. While the actual wording of the amendment is murky, proponents of what is called the 'collective' interpretation argued that the first two phrases ('A well regulated Militia, being necessary to the security of a free State…') added up to a rationale for the clause that followed ('…the right of the people to keep and bear Arms, shall not be infringed'). Since the purpose of a right to bear arms was to promote the goal of 'a well regulated militia', then it followed that activities that did not contribute to that end were not constitutionally protected. Government, as a result, was free to regulate guns as much as it wished when it came to hunting, individual self-defence, and all other uses except those having to do with the popular state militias dating from the Revolutionary War – militias, conveniently enough, that had all been incorporated in subsequent years into a section of the armed forces known as the National Guard. The right to bear arms meant the right to enlist in a portion of the US military, no more and no less.

End of argument, or so it seemed. But then the liberal edifice began to crack in 1989 when an otherwise liberal law professor named Sanford Levinson published an article in the prestigious Yale Law Review saying in so many words, 'Not so fast!' The liberal interpretation, he argued, was a case of wishful thinking, a fundamentally anachronistic reading of the amendment as well-groomed judges and academics would like it to be rather than the rough and woolly beast it really was. The post-Levinson school of thought, by now so well established that it is known as 'the standard model', holds that the real history of the amendment is more interesting and complex. American revolutionaries were creatures of an eighteenth-century school of Anglo-American thought that, aghast at the massive corruption and centralisation of power that was taking place in London, developed a kind of Manichean theory of politics in which history was seen as an endless struggle between the forces of liberty and tyranny, between virtue and corruption, and between honest country patriots and foppish courtiers who were continually trying to monopolize the reins of power. While not rejecting government outright, patriots insisted that political power was so intrinsically dangerous that it had to be checked and balanced at every turn. The legislative branch had to check the executive, while the two houses of Parliament or Congress had to check each other, and so on. The ultimate check, however, was the one not only provided by the people at large, but by a people in arms, afire with the love of liberty and determined not to relinquish one iota of its rights.

Ideas like these were ubiquitous. As early as the sixteenth century, Machiavelli had written that a virtuous people could defend liberty only by keeping itself strong and independent, well armed and well-versed in the arts of war. Sir Walter Raleigh warned that the first goal of a would-be tyrant was to 'unarm his people of weapons, money, and all means whereby they may resist his power', while the seventeenth-century political theorist James Harrington stressed the importance of an armed yeomanry composed of self-sufficient small farmers. In the late eighteenth century, James Burgh, another writer in this long 'republican' tradition, advised that 'No kingdom can be secured [against tyranny] other than by arming the people. The possession of arms is the distinction between a freeman and a slave.'

This was the patriotic myth in all its glory, one based on an idealised portrait of sturdy, self-sufficient republicans who called no man master, equated freedom and independence, and were willing to fight on behalf of either or both. What was no more than a political ideal in the old country, moreover, was practical policy in the New World where a gun was as much an everyday implement as an axe or a plough. A law passed by the Plymouth colony in 1623 in what is now Massachusetts required 'that every freeman or other inhabitant of this colony provide for himselfe and each under him able to beare arms a sufficient musket and other serviceable peece for war.' A 1639 law in Newport, Rhode Island, ordered that 'noe man shall go two miles from the Towne unarmed, eyther with Gunn or Sword; and that none shall come to any public Meeting without his weapon.' Love of liberty, self-defence, independence, old-time republican virtue – in America, such things went hand in hand. The more free men, musket in hand, succeeded in carving homes out of the wilderness, the more determined to hold onto their freedoms they became.

Ideals like these, however, took a battering in the Revolutionary War of 1775-83 in which rag-tag volunteer militias proved no substitute for a well-trained professional army. Nonetheless, in order to win ratification of a new Constitution in 1787-88, Washington, his former aide-de-camp Alexander Hamilton, and other top Federalists agreed to a Second Amendment enshrining the concept of a people in arms. Even if they regarded popular militias as militarily valueless, they figured that no harm could come of summer patriots drilling in the village square. A half-century before the

advent of the first professional police forces, no one imagined the threat that an unchecked proliferation of private weapons might pose to public safety.

Assuming they've made it this far, readers outside the US may be forgiven for scratching their heads and saying, 'So what?' Interesting as all this may or may not be, what do Machiavelli, Raleigh, et al. have to do with modern policy? If it is difficult to imagine a member of the British, French, or German government scrutinising the words of some eighteenth-century politician for guidance about how to craft a modern gun-control policy, why does it come so naturally to Americans?

But this is precisely the point. In a democracy, supposedly, the people rule. Therefore, if the people believe that tighter gun controls are what society needs, the people should get them. The problem, however, is that the Constitution – the source, as we have seen, of all political and legal authority in the US – allows as few as thirteen states out of fifty, representing as little as 4.5 percent of the population, to block any constitutional change, no matter how modest. The adoption of a bit of corrective language explaining what, precisely, 'a well regulated militia' is supposed to mean, or whether a 'right to bear arms' implies that every citizen is entitled to his or her own rocket launcher, would go a long way toward clearing up the confusion. Yet given the sheer immobility of the Constitution and everything in it, clarification will not be forthcoming. Despite polls showing a consistent 60 to 70 percent majority in favour of stricter gun control, the law as presently written in all its unfathomable glory will prevail. As long as sentiment among academics and members of Congress continues to run in favour of a more expansive reading of the Second Amendment, serious gun control will remain out of the question. The democratic majority will find itself stymied by a two-century-old constitutional amendment that 'we the people' made, but which 'we the people' can no longer change.

This explains the American political system's deep structural bias against gun control. Where the great fear among the men who drew up the Constitution was of a popularly elected legislature falling over itself to do the public's bidding, the spectacle post-Columbine was of a popularly elected body falling over itself not to carry out the democratic will.

This also explains the look of proud defiance on the faces of so many of Zed Nelson's subjects. Gun owners in the United States know that they are unpopular. They are aware that public opinion is running against them. But they don't care. As long as they have the Constitution, America's ancient charter of liberty, on their side, silly things like democratic opinion do not matter. Besides, a good republican is supposed to stand fast against the popular tide. If modernity is marked by corruption, tyranny, and endless fads and fashions, then the patriot's job is to hold tight to plain, old-fashioned values.

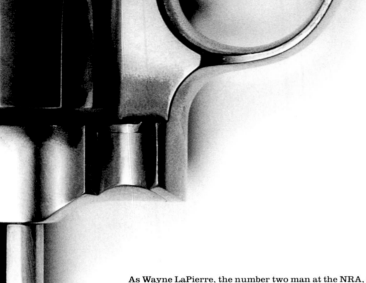

As Wayne LaPierre, the number two man at the NRA, said of left-wing intellectuals who criticise the Constitution:

What they really want is to redefine freedom in this country. And they want to redefine the way we structure our rights in this country. They think they're more powerful than the single most powerful declaration of freedom in the history of the world. They are arrogant. They think they have better ideas and they are smarter than Thomas Jefferson, James Madison, Tom Paine, Patrick Henry, George Mason.

A real patriot, aware that true greatness lies in the past, knows that no one today can hold a candle to such Eighteenth-century giants and that Americans, consequently, must subordinate themselves to their dictates.

America is thus a counter-democracy, one in which the people are free to speak their mind and their ramshackle, pre-modern form of government is free to ignore them. The number of privately owned weapons in the US, estimated at around 250 million as of the year 2000, continues to rise by 5 to 7 million per year. Liberal politicians, trying to reconcile the irreconcilable, continue to trot out ridiculous proposals to ban some kinds of firearms but not others, to limit handgun purchases to one a month, or to provide for three-day waiting periods so that the authorities can determine whether or not a would-be purchaser is a homicidal maniac – anything and everything, in other words, to avoid challenging head on both the gun culture and the Second Amendment on which it rests. Instead of serious action, politicians find it easier to fulminate against lurid video games and theatre owners who allow sixteen-year-olds to see adult films. The moral seems to be that guns don't kill people – R-rated movies do.

This is absurd, yet everything in American culture is designed to cover up such absurdity with a thick layer of constitutional piety. 'When we are lost, the best thing to do is to look to our Constitution as a beacon of light and a guide to get us through trying times.' So sang Representative Zoe Lofgren, a California Democrat, when Congress was debating Bill Clinton's impeachment in 1998. 'The Constitution provides a path to follow in these circumstances,' added Asa Hutchinson, an Arkansas Republican. 'It may be well worn, but it is well marked, and we would be wise to follow it rather than to concoct our own ideas on how to proceed.' It is better to rely on the Founders, in other words, than to think for ourselves. Since the democratic majority can't change the Second Amendment, it has no choice but to live with it. But since this means standing by while ordinary people are gunned down by a seemingly endless succession of heavily-armed maniacs, it is increasingly unable to do so. The flip side of the unbounded faith of a Zoe Lofgren or an Asa Hutchinson is utter paralysis in the face of a law that is simultaneously intractable and obsolete, and a modern problem that won't go away.

Contrary to America's 'civil religion,' the 55 merchants, lawyers, and slave-owners who created the Constitution in 1787 were not supermen, but ordinary mortals who thought they were creating a form of government that, if they were lucky, would last for years or maybe even decades. No one thought in terms of centuries – indeed, how could they? Yet the fact that the plan of government they devised has lasted so long forces Americans to grapple with a question concerning their obligation to the past. Because the Founders settled on a certain balance between freedom and order, does that mean that latter-day US citizens are obliged to follow suit? Or are they free to strike a different balance? Times change. From a string of coastal settlements, the United States has grown into a republic of 270 million people stretching across the entire North American continent. It is a congested, polluted society filled with traffic jams, shopping malls, and anomic suburbs in which an eighteenth-century right to bear arms is as out of place as silk knee-britches and tricornered hats. So why must we Americans subordinate ourselves to an ancient law that, if the latest scholarship is correct, is contrary to what the democratic majority believes is in its best interest? Why can't we create the kind of society we want rather than the one the Founders bestowed upon us? The Founders are dead and buried and will not be around to suffer the consequences. We the living will.

There is simply no solution to the gun problem within the confines of the US Constitution. To most Americans, trained from childhood to regard the Constitution as a form of holy writ, a statement like this will sound strange, if not incomprehensible. As one well-known constitutional scholar put it in the pages of the Harvard Law Review, the Constitution serves to 'structure the conversation of ordinary Americans as they ponder the most fundamental and sometimes divisive issues in our republic.' What this means, in essence, is that the Constitution's domination of US society is so complete that it controls the way Americans discuss and debate, even the way we think. Americans are unable to conceive of an alternative framework, to think 'outside the box', as the corporate strategists put it. Other countries are free to change their constitutions. In fact, with the exception of Great Britain, there is not a single advanced industrial nation that has not thoroughly revamped its constitution since 1945. If they can do it, why can't we? Why must Americans remain slaves to the past?

Daniel Lazare, July 2000

Daniel Lazare is the author of
The Frozen Republic: How the Constitution Is Paralyzing Democracy
(Harcourt Brace, 1996).

AN ARMED SOCIETY
IS A POLITE SOCIETY.

POLICE OFFICER TOM PERRETT, 52.

WITH A BIBLE IN ONE HAND AND A GUN IN THE OTHER, WE CAN MAKE THIS COUNTRY ONE NATION UNDER GOD ONCE AGAIN.

RICHARD MACK – FORMER ARIZONA SHERIFF. FIRST SHERIFF IN THE US TO FILE A LAWSUIT
AGAINST THE FEDERAL GOVERNMENT IN OPPOSITION TO THE GUN-CONTROL BRADY BILL.

This is called a 'belly-gun'.
It's just a colloquialism.
You stick it in the belly and pull the trigger.
You can't miss them that way…

GARY HARDIN, VIETNAM VETERAN AND GUN SALESMAN.

A GUN

ND AMENDMENT

"You do not know you need it
they come to take it away."
Thomas Jefferson

't Kill People

Kill People

In the Ten Commandments the actual Hebrew is not, 'Thou Shalt Not Kill'.
It is, in fact, 'Thou Shalt Not Murder'. So this, as far as we're concerned, is self-defence.

John and Kaywin LeNoue, Born Again Christians.

Have you ever seen them crack a chest?
It's like a hog slaughter.
Patricia Artella, paramedic.

IT'S MY CONSTITUTIONAL RIGHT TO OWN A GUN AND PROTECT MY FAMILY.

Mike. Father and gun owner.

Sure I would unload my gun on someone; not because I want to hurt them, but because I'm going to make sure they're down. That's what the course teaches you; to empty the clip.
Elizabeth Strong, 28.

I'll be carrying a 9mm semi-automatic from now on. Things are getting dangerous out there. I hope and pray that the person I shoot doesn't die; that'd be great, but I'm goin' to shoot so that I don't die.
Susan Wilson, 44.

People in this country huddle in their houses and throw the dead-bolts, but I will not succumb to the scum that is out there.
Vicky Sykes, 40.

I got a .410 shotgun from Santa Claus last year.

Sarah Read, age 10.

For more information, contact your local dealer.

TANNER FIRST FIRED A GUN AGED THREE.
HE NOW OWNS A .243 RUGER RIFLE, A REMINGTON .58
AND A .20-GAUGE AUTOMATIC SHOTGUN.

JACK CONE WITH SONS ANDREW, 10, AND TANNER, 12.

Every day I look at this and think,
'Hey, anybody could own one of these…'
That's why you gotta fight fire with fire.

DOUG TWEDEY AND SCOTT.

B&B'S GUN STORE – HOLLYWOOD, LOS ANGELES.
Sales increased following the widely publicised
North Hollywood shootout, where Los Angeles police
officers were outgunned by two heavily- armed bank
robbers wearing body-armour. A group of LAPD
officers rushed from the siege to B&B's gun store,
borrowing M-15 assault rifles and pump-action
shotguns with hundreds of rounds of ammunition,
before returning to the crime scene and killing the
besieged robbers with the unofficial firearms.
During the televised shoot-out 1,100 rounds of
ammunition were fired, nine police officers were shot
and injured, seven civilians were wounded in the
crossfire, and both bank robbers were shot dead.

We've seen just about everything. M-16 rifles, AR-15 semi-auto's, hunting rifles with homemade silencers, even an Armalite 5.56 Nato calibre assault rifle. These guns could have been used by anyone from petty criminals to big-time drug-dealers… they could have been used in robberies, domestics and homicides.

SGNT. MICHAEL RALLINS, MEMPHIS POLICE FIREARMS CENTER, WITH WEAPONS CONFISCATED FROM STREETS AND HOMES OF MEMPHIS RESIDENTS.

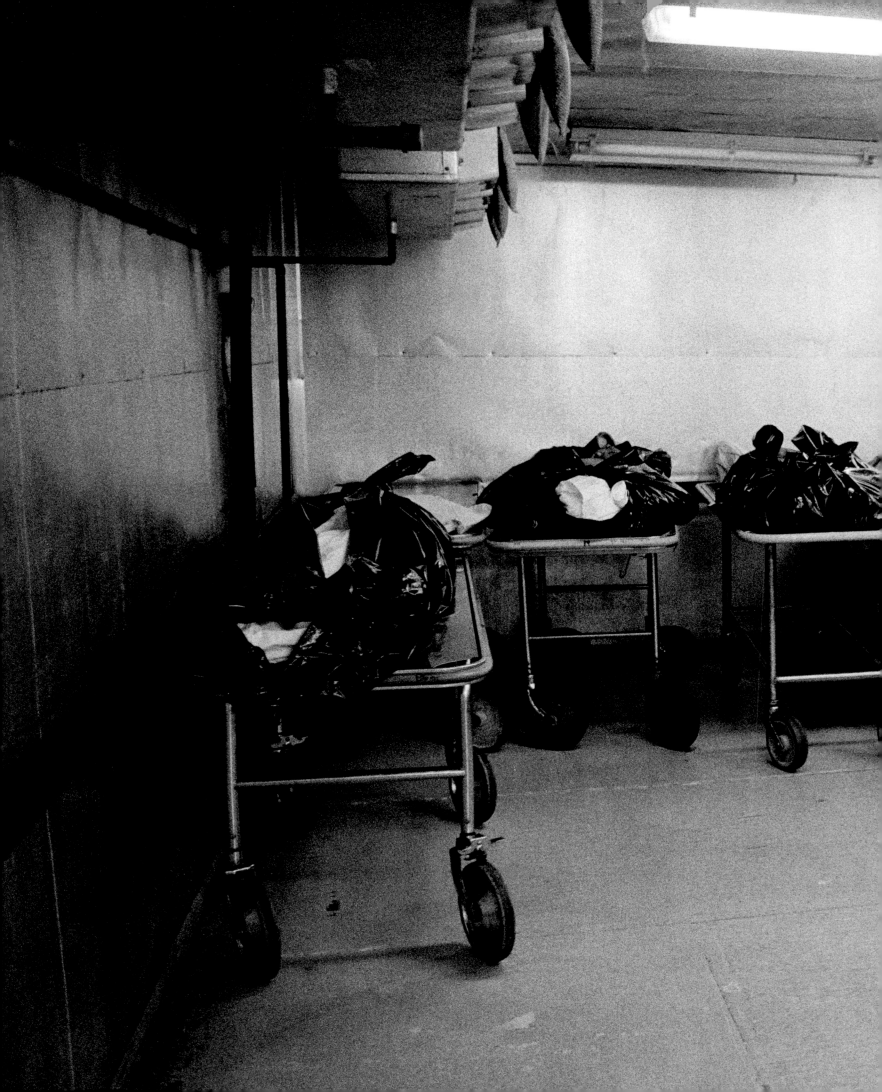

We all have this big macho thing that somebody's gonna break into our house and we're gonna be sitting there in a rocking chair with a shotgun. But in reality it ain't like that. DR GREG STANFORD, DALLAS PARKLAND HOSPITAL.

The actual semi-automatic weapons used by
the Los Angeles Police in the infamous North
Hollywood shoot-out are sold at auction with
the assistance of Melinda Clark, TV actress.
Soldier of Fortune Expo, banquet and auction,
Sands Convention Center, Las Vegas.

Police training, Las Vegas firing range.

The 'Alaskan Survival' is a gun which uses a shotgun
cartridge. If you were shot with that, that's gonna kill you...
or rather 'stop' you. You shouldn't use the word 'kill.'

Most shootings take place in domestic situations. A sizeable number of people who kill other people are so-called law-abiding citizens. The law-abiding citizen produces a lot of the fatalities, by mistake, in anger, or by accident.

Dr Francisco – Medical Examiner. Performed 9,000 autopsies since 1969, including Elvis Presley and Martin Luther King.

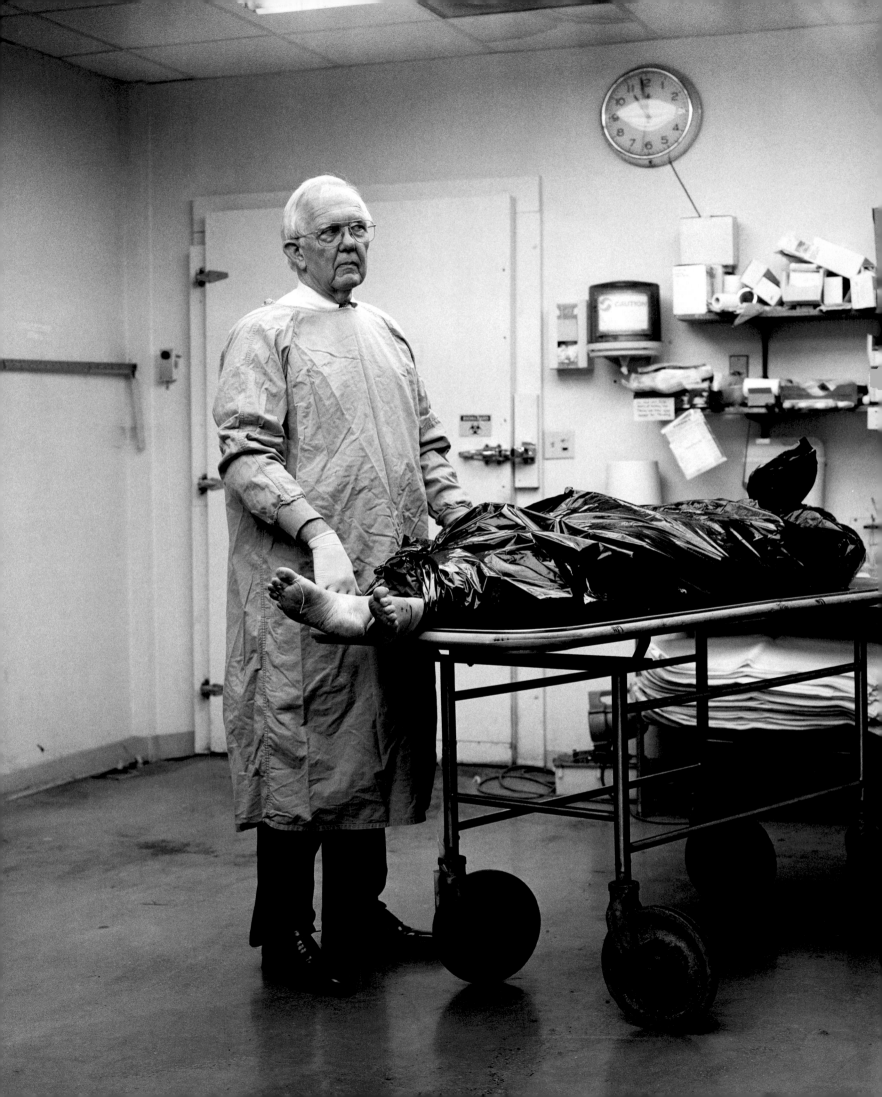

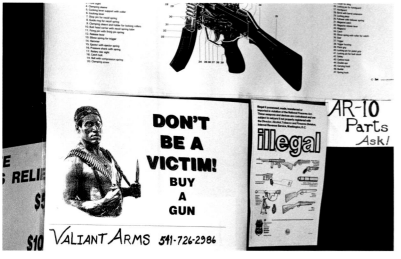

Tools used for self-defence should be available to all citizens. The Second Amendment has been interpreted by the US Supreme Court to mean the tools available to mankind at the time, no matter what that time is. And the more advanced those tools get, then they should still be available to the average person in the population.

Steve Shreiner, Soldier of Fortune, CEO.

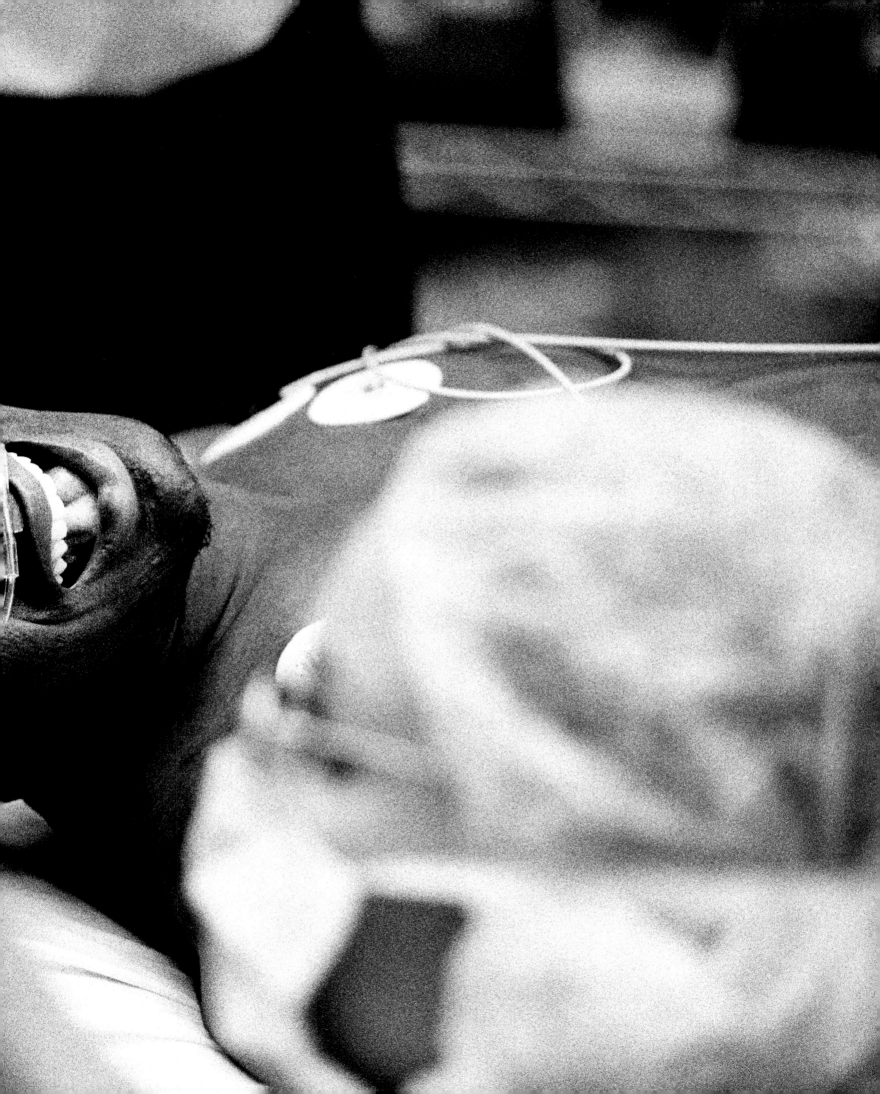

IT'S NOT NECESSARILY A MAN-STOPPER, BUT I WOULD NOT WANNA BE SHOT WITH IT.

Sandy Chisholm, President of North American Arms Inc. Miniature handgun, $150.

Retirement gifts – a high-powered rifle and a bouquet of roses – are presented
to a long serving employee at the Soldier of Fortune annual convention.
SANDS CONVENTION CENTER, LAS VEGAS.

KEEP YOUR ASSULT RIFLES CLEAN $1.⁰⁰ ♥

...ORIGINAL... COORS ♡ (you know, the beer company) CRUCIBLES

Prospective buyer. National Rifle Association
annual convention and gun show. Dallas.

**WOULD YOU LIKE TO HAVE YOUR WIFE
COME TO THE MORGUE TO IDENTIFY
YOU, OR WOULD YOU RATHER GO AND
STAND BEFORE A JUDGE AND TELL
HIM WHY YOU WERE CARRYING A GUN?**

GUN SALESMAN, SMITTY'S SPORTING GOODS, DALLAS.

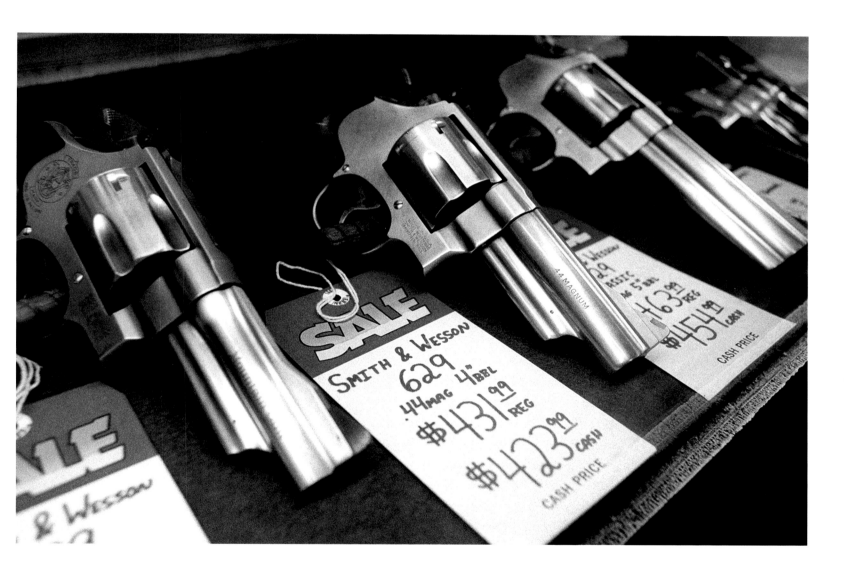

Honeymoon couple, Las Vegas.

DANIEL GREEN, 21. GUNSHOT TO THIGH. 11.30PM SATURDAY NIGHT.
SHOT BY FRIEND AFTER DRUNKEN ARGUMENT WITH .45 CALIBRE HANDGUN.

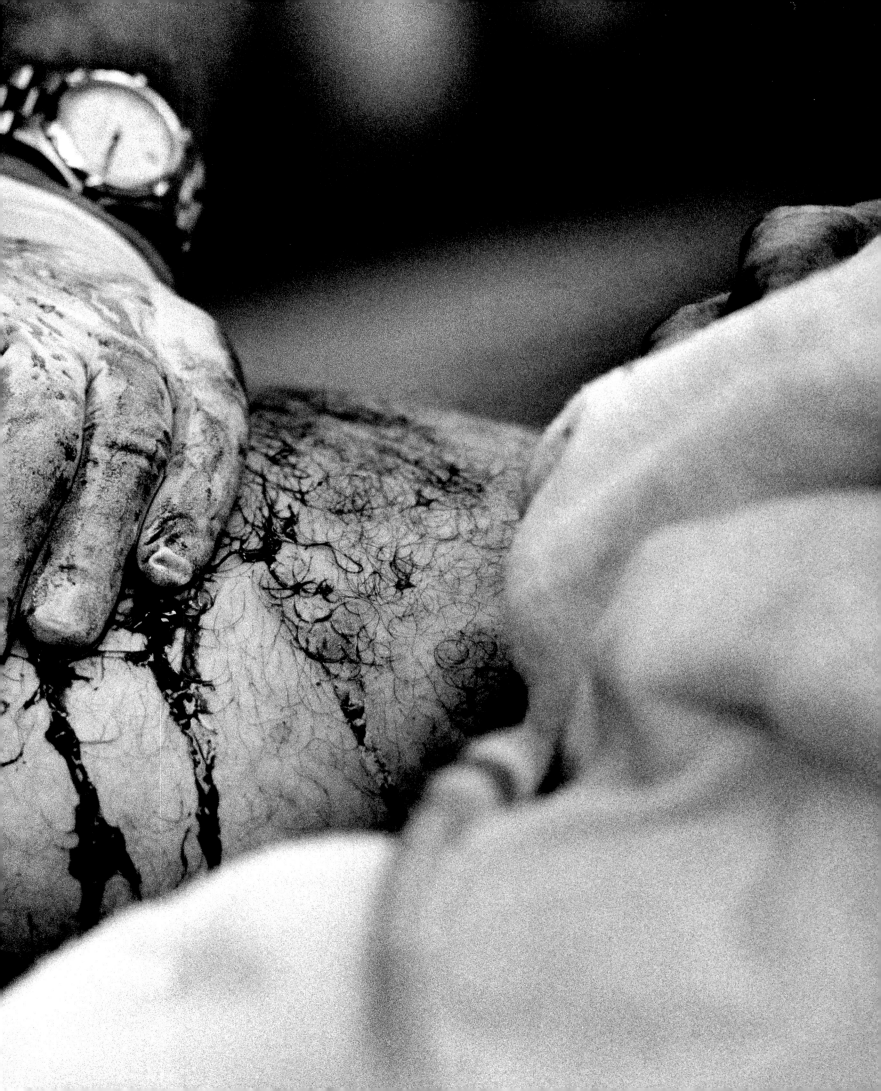

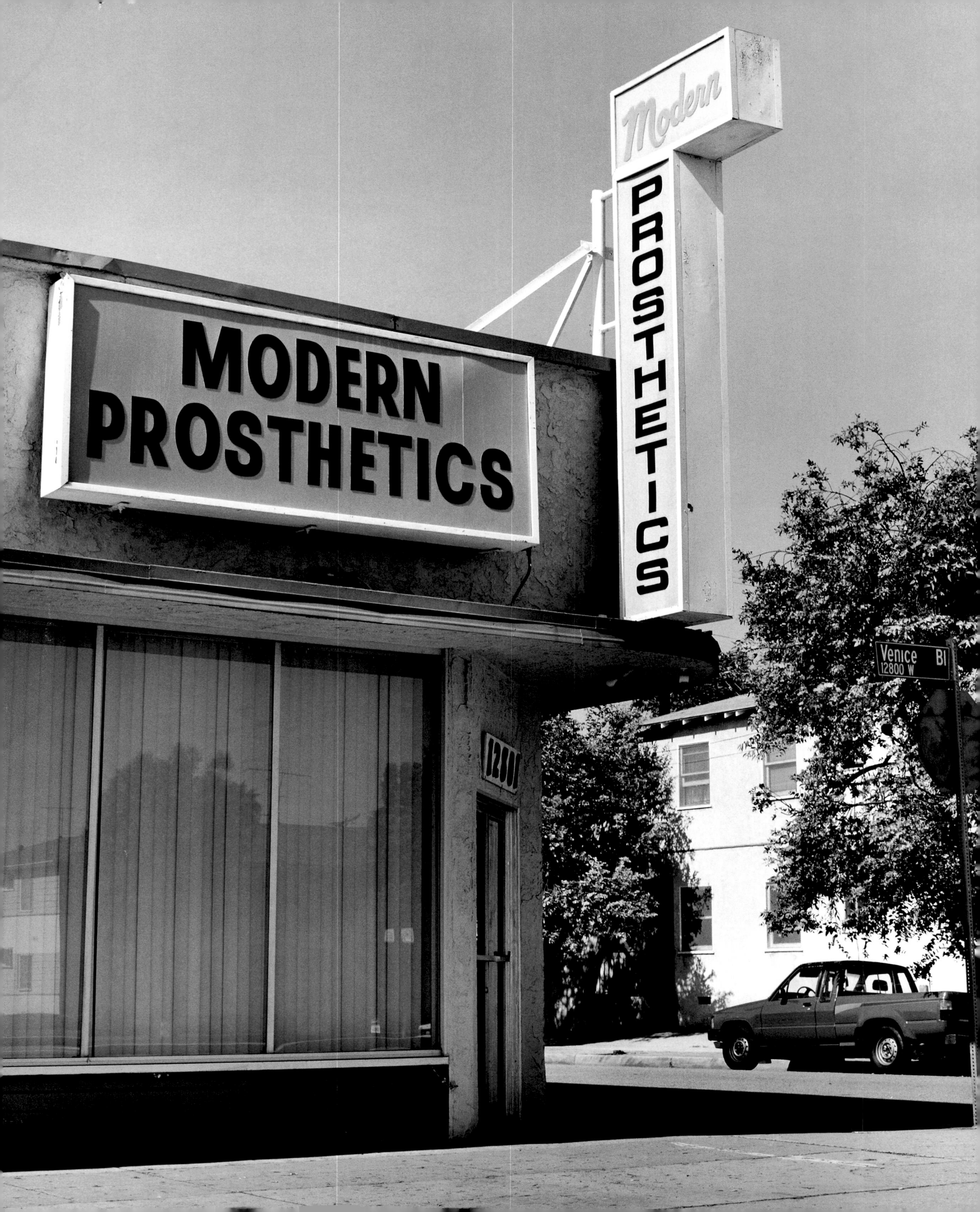

MODERN
PROSTHETICS

Modern

PROSTHETICS

12800

Venice Bl
12800 W

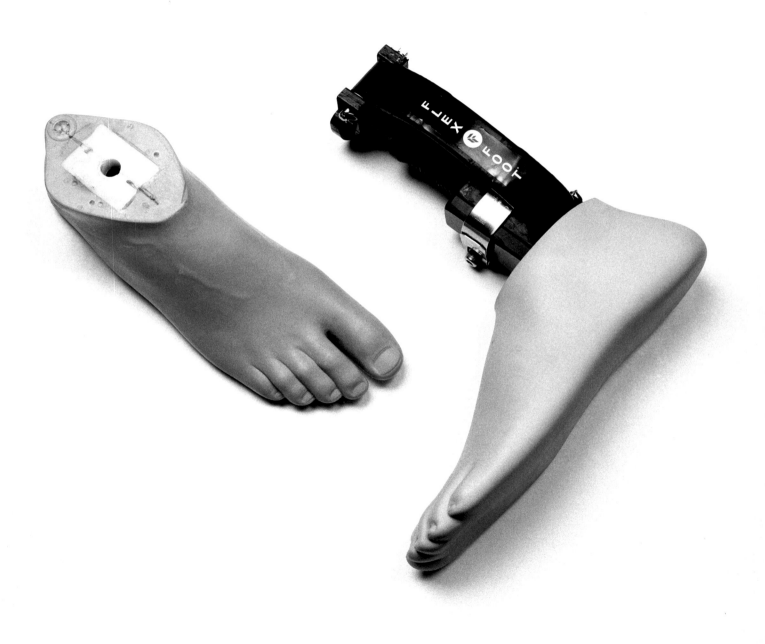

5% of my clients are here as a result of gunshots.

Edward 'Skip' Martin. Precision Prosthetics. Artificial foot, $1,500.

I SHOT MYSELF WHILE I WAS CLEANING MY HUNTING RIFLE... I THOUGHT IT WAS UNLOADED.

You hear about that young guy who brought a sawn-off shotgun to his girlfriend's to show off? When he pulled it out from his belt he blew his whacker clean off! The whole damn lot!

GRADY C. HINTON, 46. FREELANCE MORTICIAN. LEG AMPUTEE.

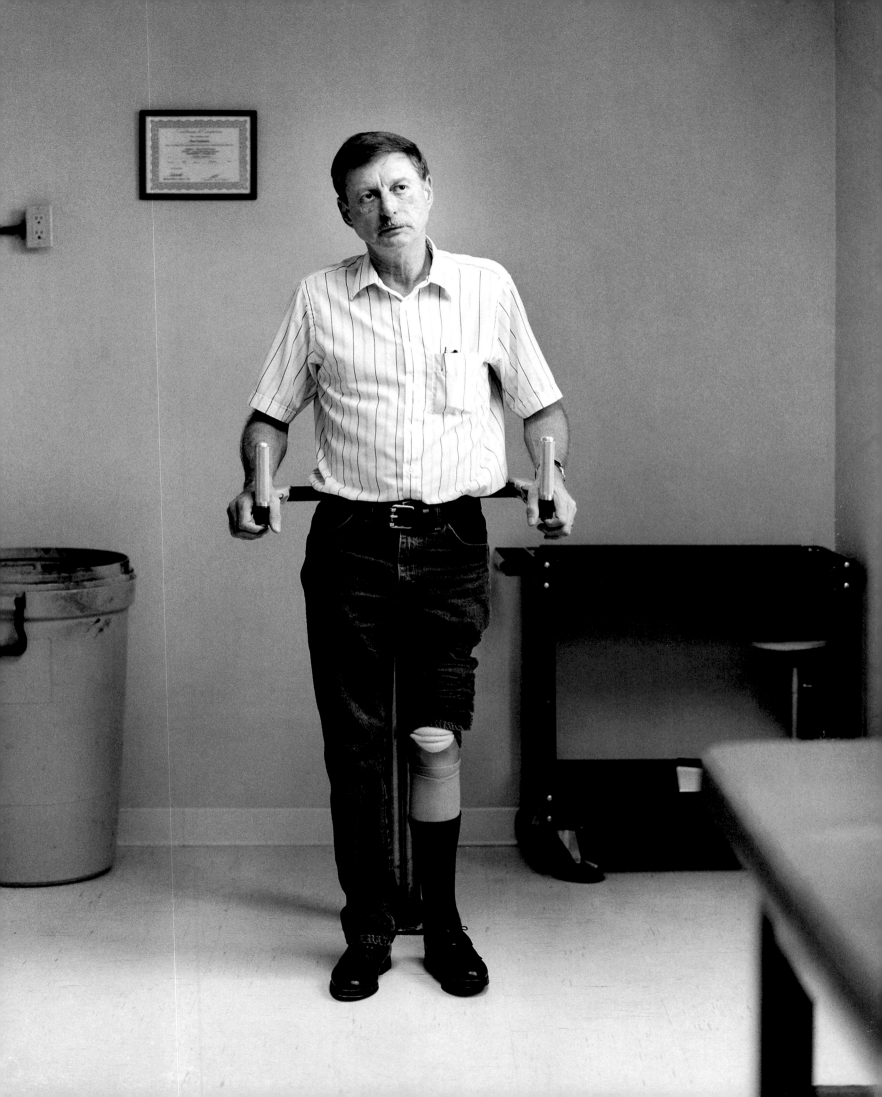

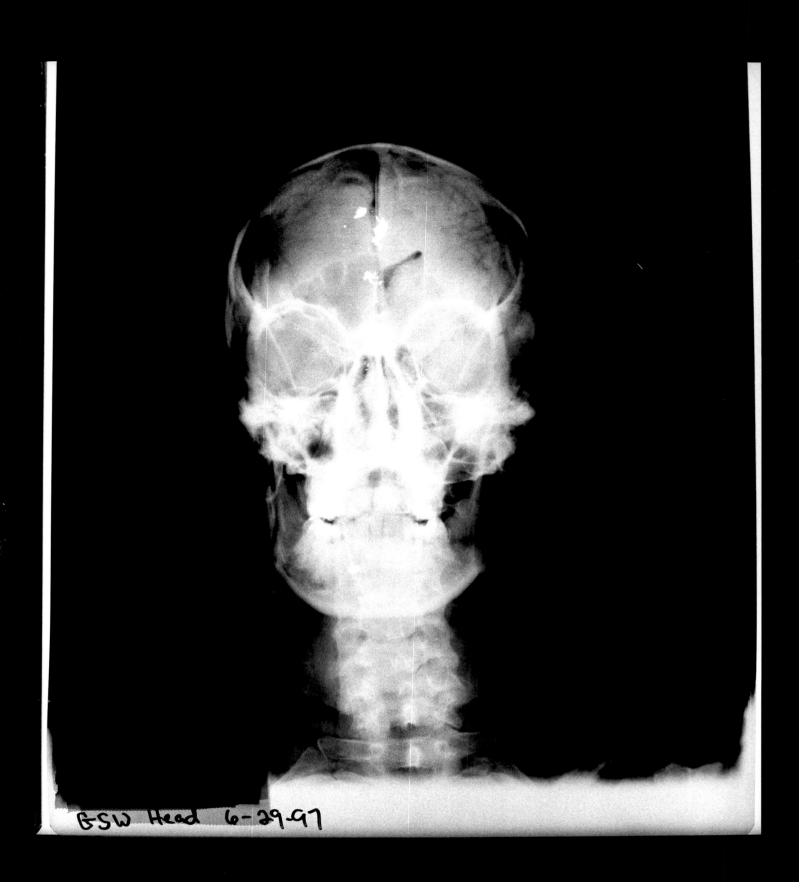

GSW Head 6-29-97

X-RAY OF SUICIDE VICTIM. GUN-SHOT WOUND TO HEAD.

Those most likely to commit suicide are white middle-aged men.
There are more gun-related suicides every year in the US than
gun-related homicides.

AMERICA'S AMMUNITION OF CHOICE – THE HOLLOW-POINT BULLET, DESIGNED TO MAXIMISE CAVITATIONAL DAMAGE BY 'MUSHROOMING' AND FRAGMENTING ON IMPACT. BANNED FROM USE IN WAR BY THE GENEVA CONVENTION.

Ambulance paramedics deliver the fifth gunshot victim of the
night to the roof of the Elvis Presley Trauma Centre, Memphis.

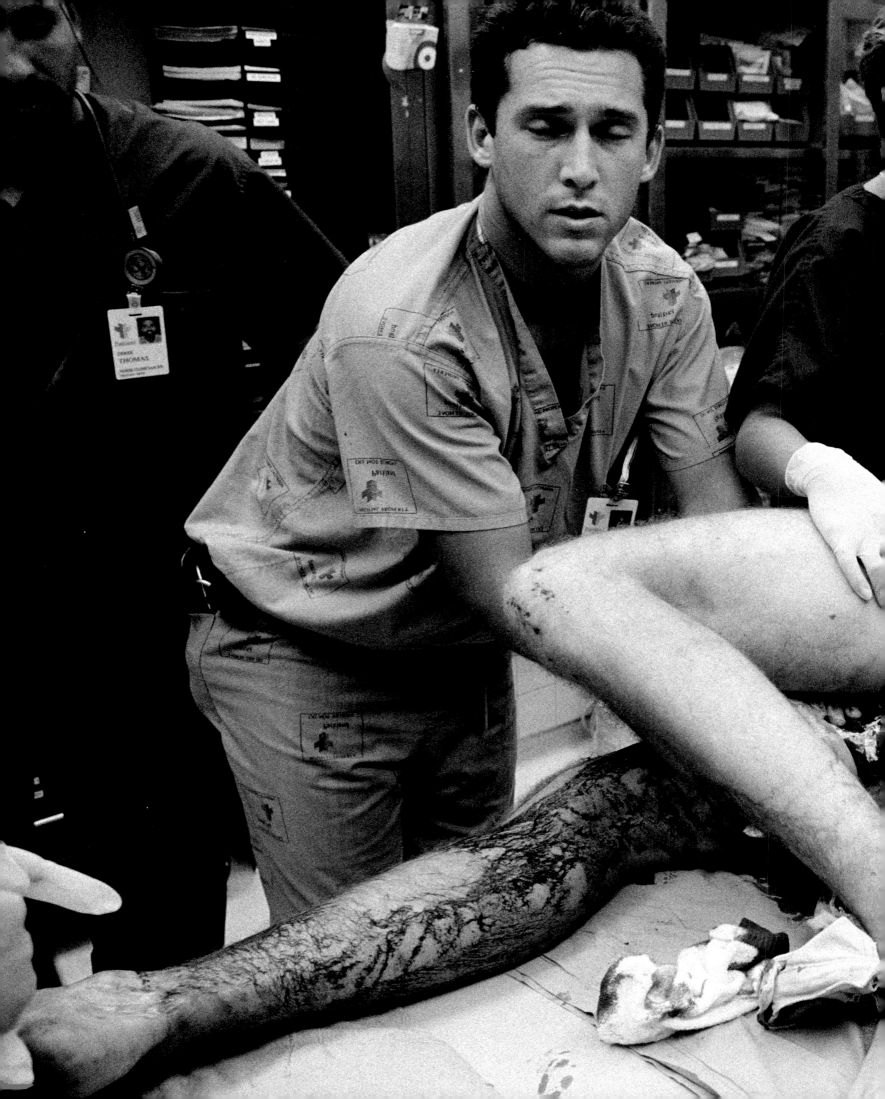

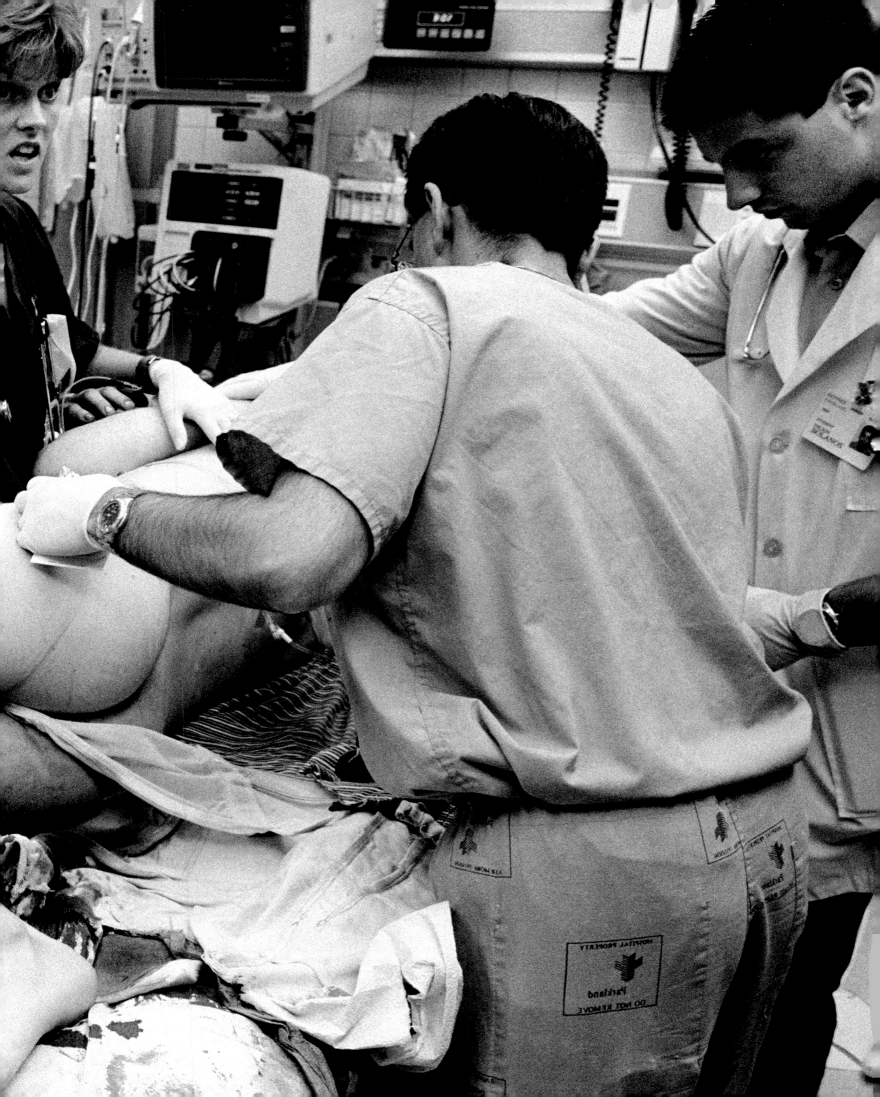

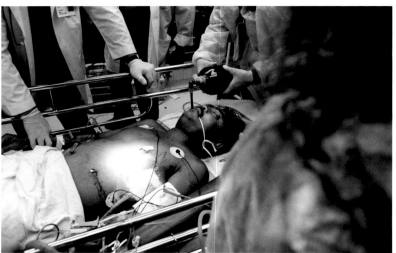
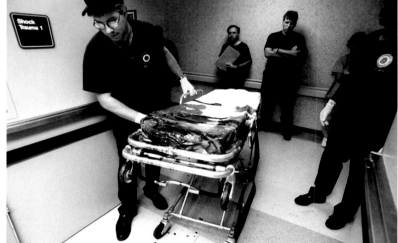

We tubed him, bagged him, put him on an EKG heart monitor, put in two large-bore IV's, suctioned a bunch of snot out of his throat, raised his feet. He had no pulse, we were breathing for him... I'd say he was hangin' on by a thread.
Bubba Atkinson, ambulance paramedic.

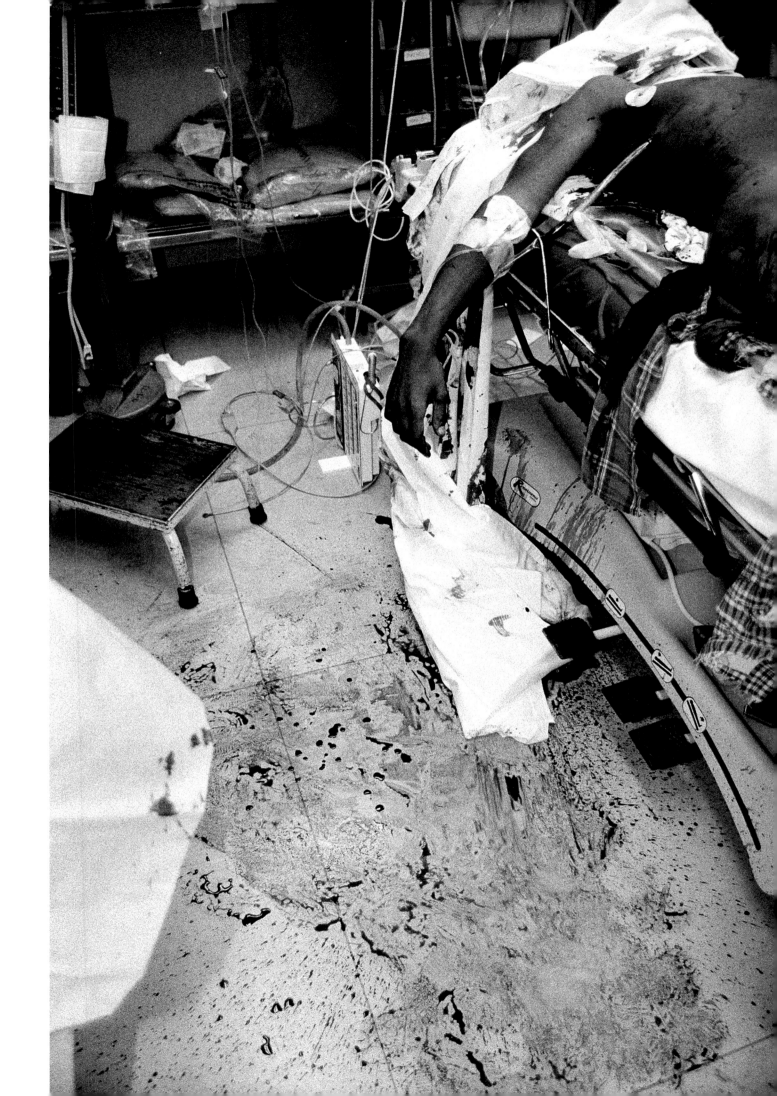

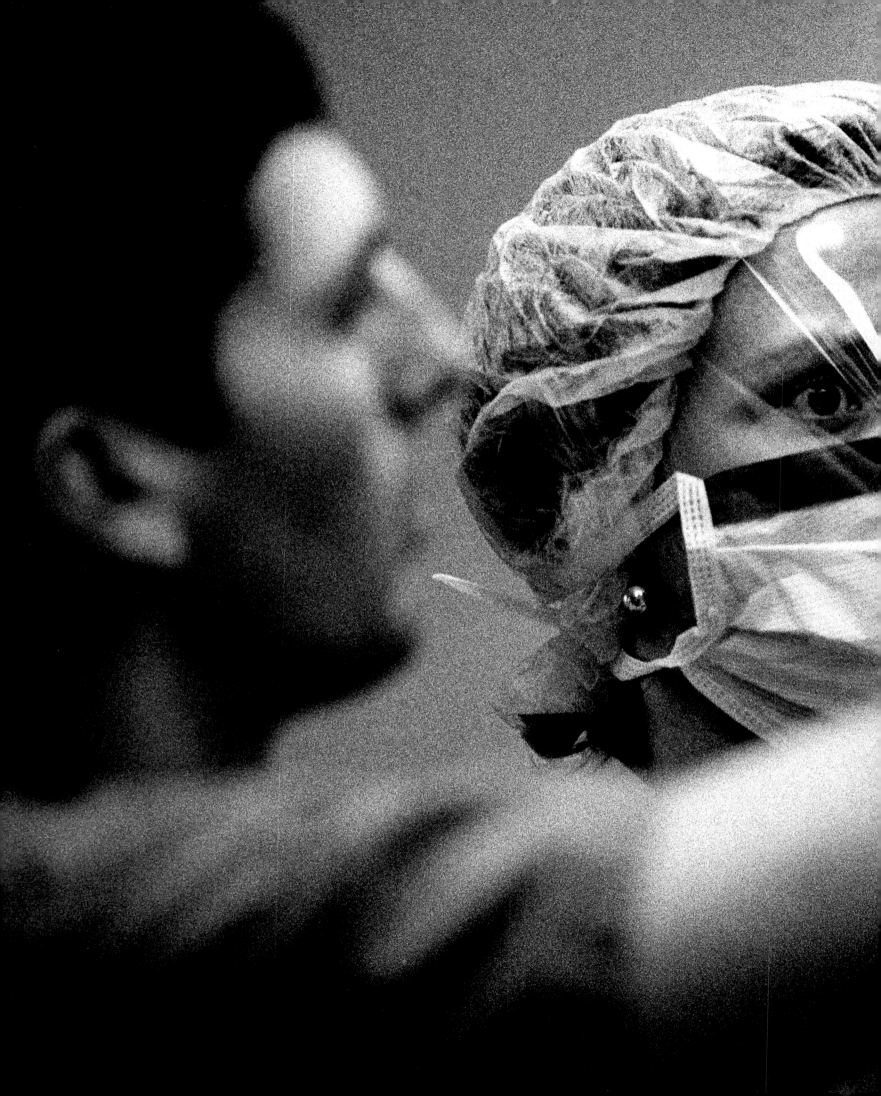

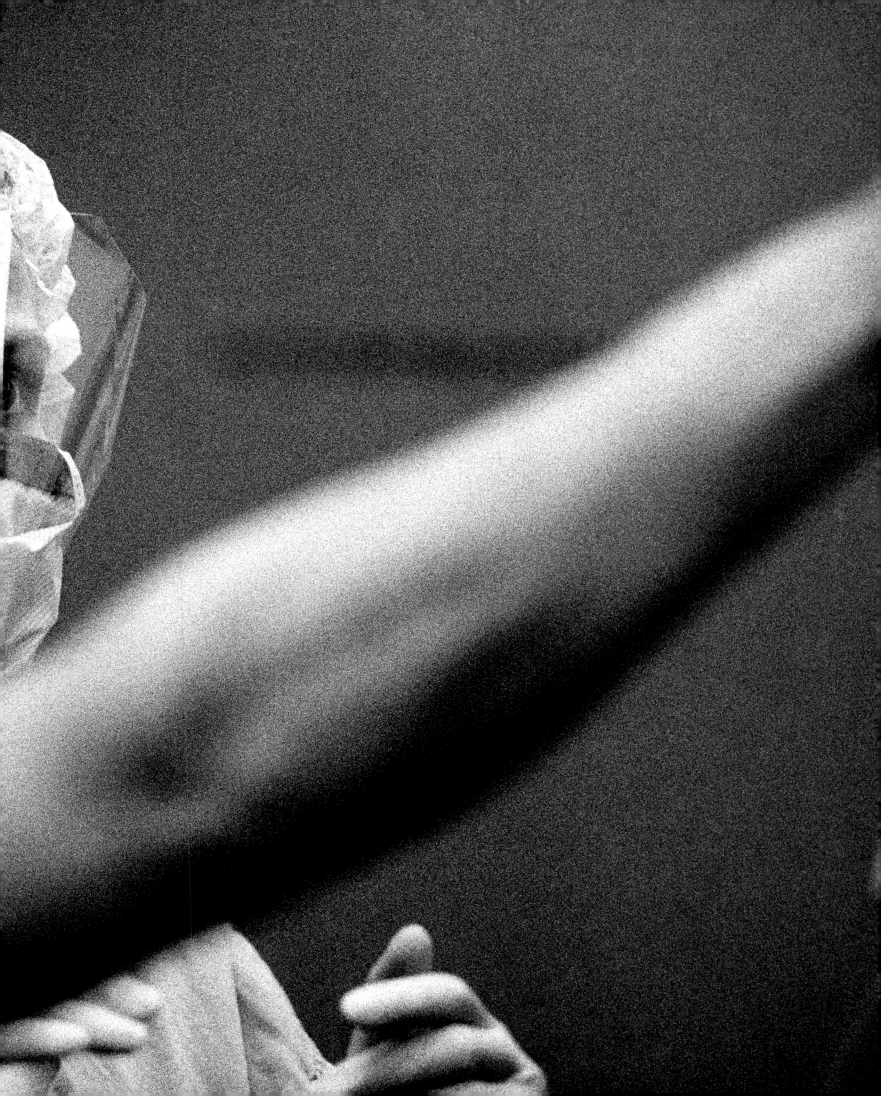

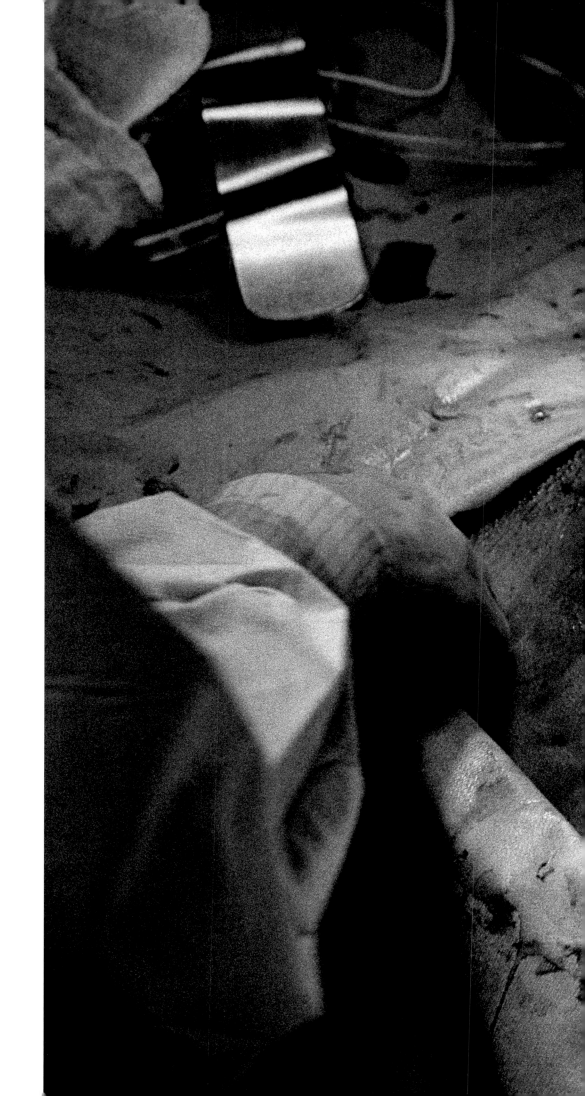

A round from an AK-47 assault rifle leaves the muzzle at 2,300 feet per second, twice the speed of sound. When it hits a person, the density of the tissue forces the round to yaw to one side until it is travelling sideways, or even backwards. Shock waves ripple through the tissue and create a cavity that can be as much as eleven times the size of the bullet. The cavity lasts only a few thousandths of a second, but the shock waves that created it can shred organs that the bullet never even touches. In head wounds, the temporary cavity is particularly devastating because the skull – being rigid – can only respond to the sudden deformation by bursting.
PARAMEDIC, DALLAS PARKLAND HOSPITAL.

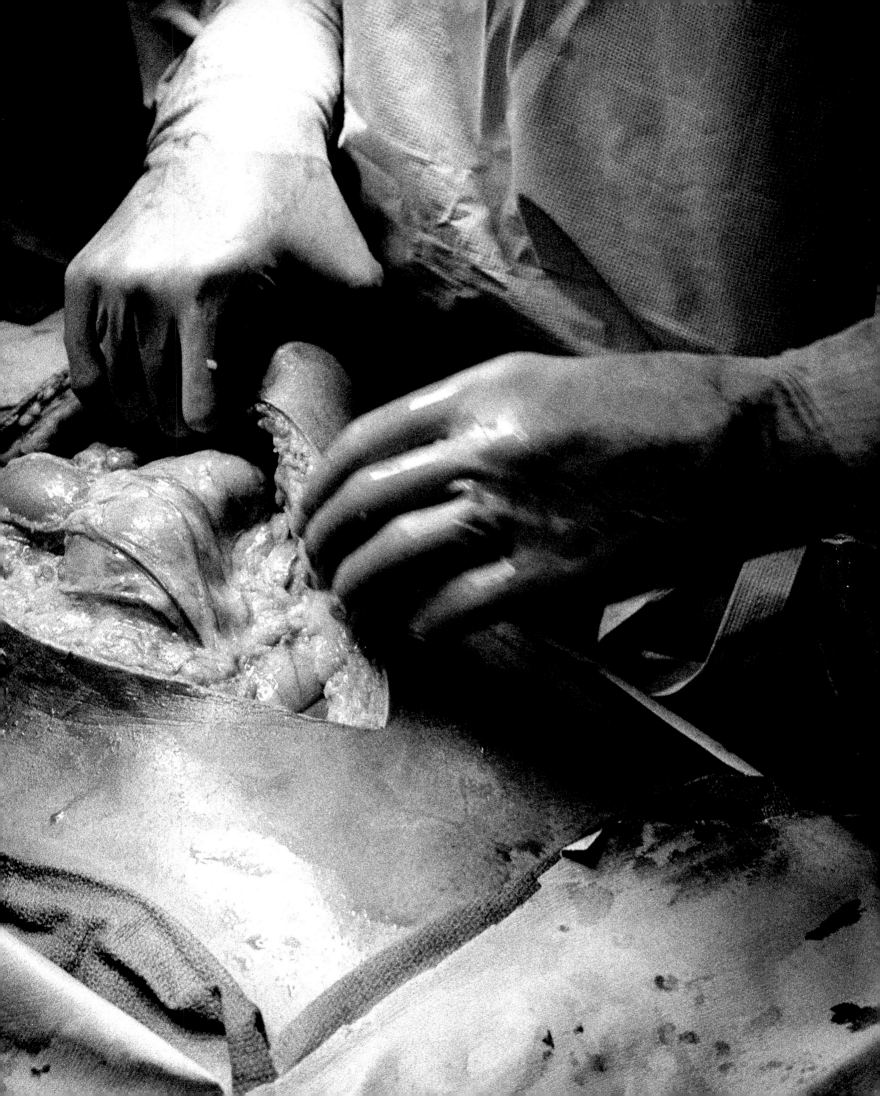

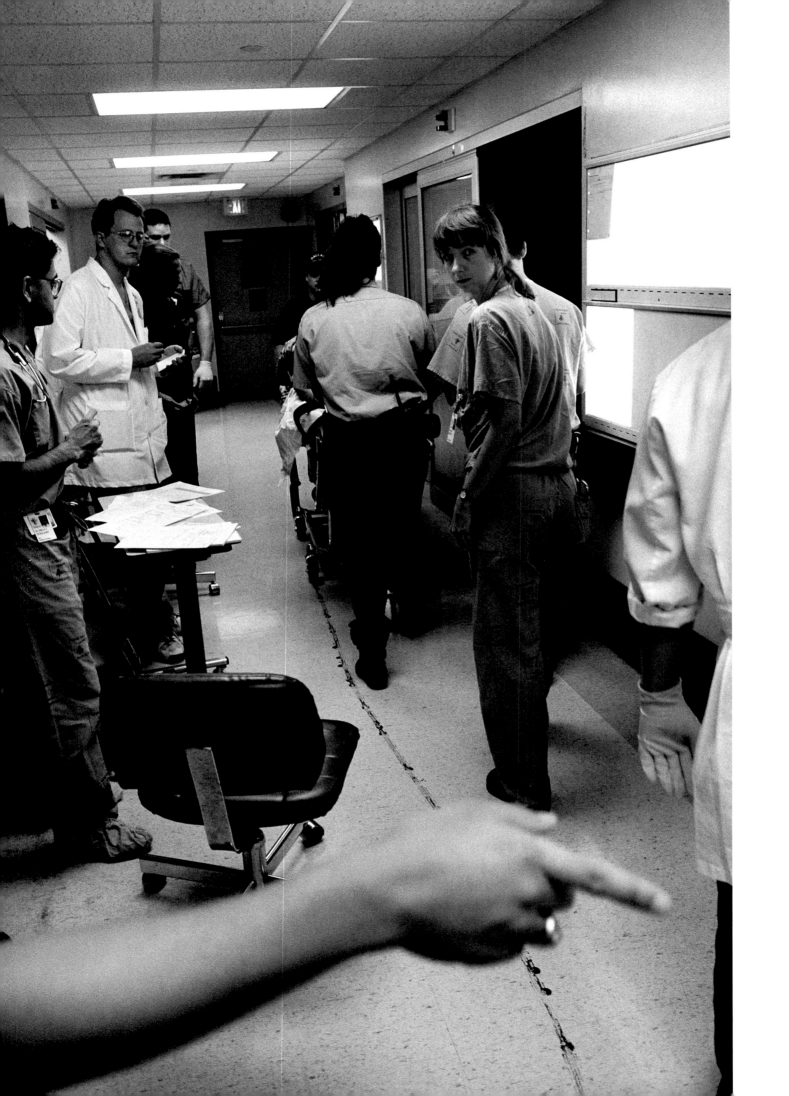

Gunshot victim is wheeled into the emergency room of Dallas Parkland Hospital, where President Kennedy was rushed following his assassin's bullet.

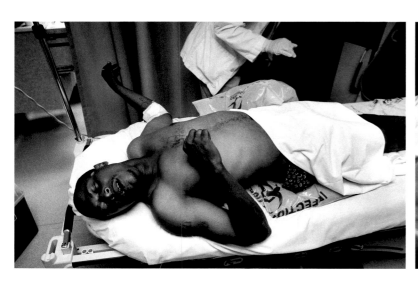
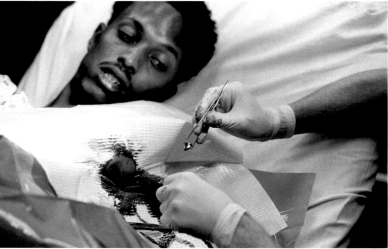

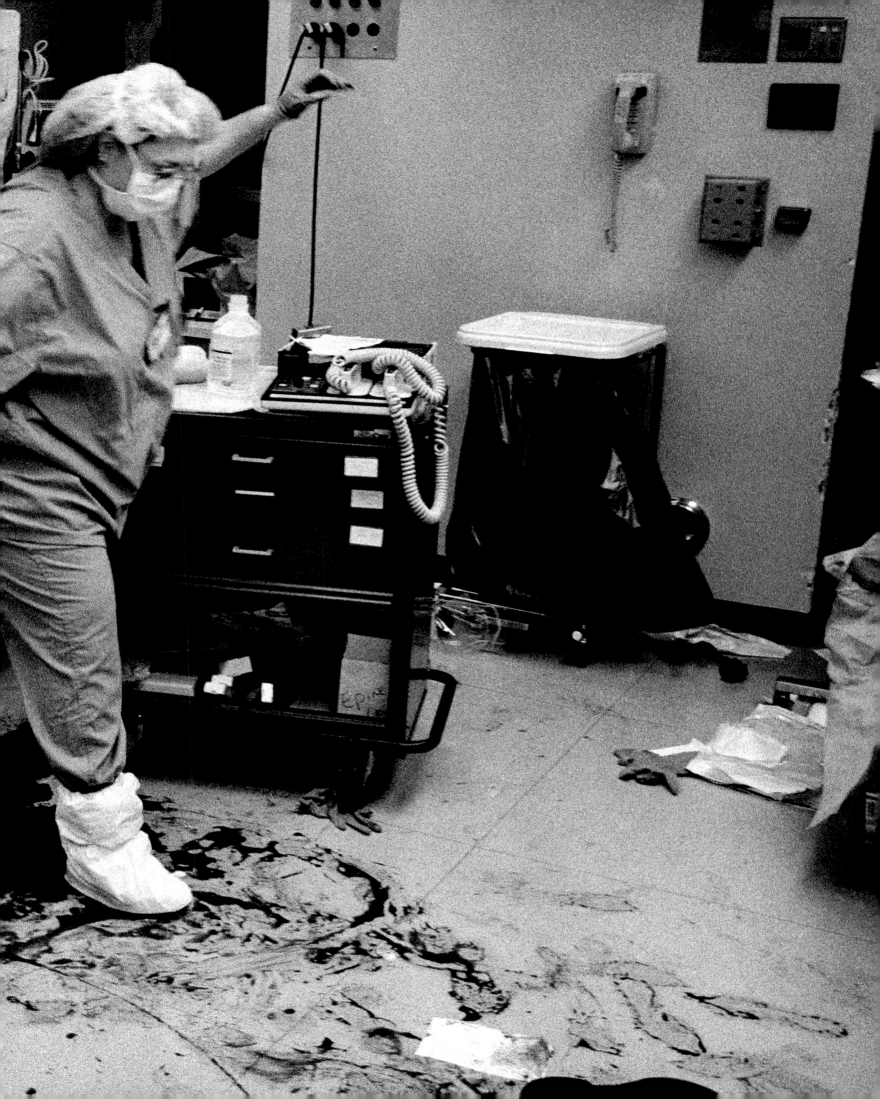

WE THOUGHT WE WERE IN THE SAFEST PLACE IN AMERICA.

Grandparents of fourteen year-old Kayce Steger,
one of four children shot to death at Heath High
School by a classmate wearing ear-plugs and armed
with a semi-automatic handgun, a shotgun and a
hunting rifle. Paducah, Kentucky.

There's nothing worse than to wake up and be defenceless. If a person knows he can reach under his bed, pull up his .45 with his night-sights on it, and be ready to go instantly, you have the ability to defend yourself and protect your household, which I feel is your God-given right.

TOM MILLETT, PRESIDENT OF MILLETT SIGHTS.

BULLET-RIDDLED CAR.
The owner of the vehicle saw two armed young men attempting to steal his car from his driveway. He opened fire on them from his lounge with a high-velocity deer-hunting rifle, killing one man and wounding the other. Police valued the car at $900.

PEOPLE ARE PARANOID, YES, BUT IT DOESN'T
MEAN YOU'RE NOT GOING TO BECOME A VICTIM...

RESERVE POLICE OFFICER, KANSAS, SOUTH CAROLINA.

Amed Itayem
Owner, Pops Grocery Store.

MALCOLM W. GARY, 31. PRO-TECH SECURITY
GUARD. SEESALLS GROCERY STORE. MEMPHIS.
I carry a Smith & Wesson 9mm semi-automatic.
One in the chamber and fifteen in the clip; that's
sixteen bullets. It's on 'safety' right now, but
when I'm guarding a bank I don't have the safety
on. Anyway, I got him up there guarding me,
lookin' out for me.

IN A STUDY OF ACCIDENTAL HANDGUN SHOOTINGS
OF CHILDREN UNDER SIXTEEN, NEARLY 40%
OF THE SHOOTINGS OCCURRED IN THE HOMES OF
FRIENDS AND RELATIVES.

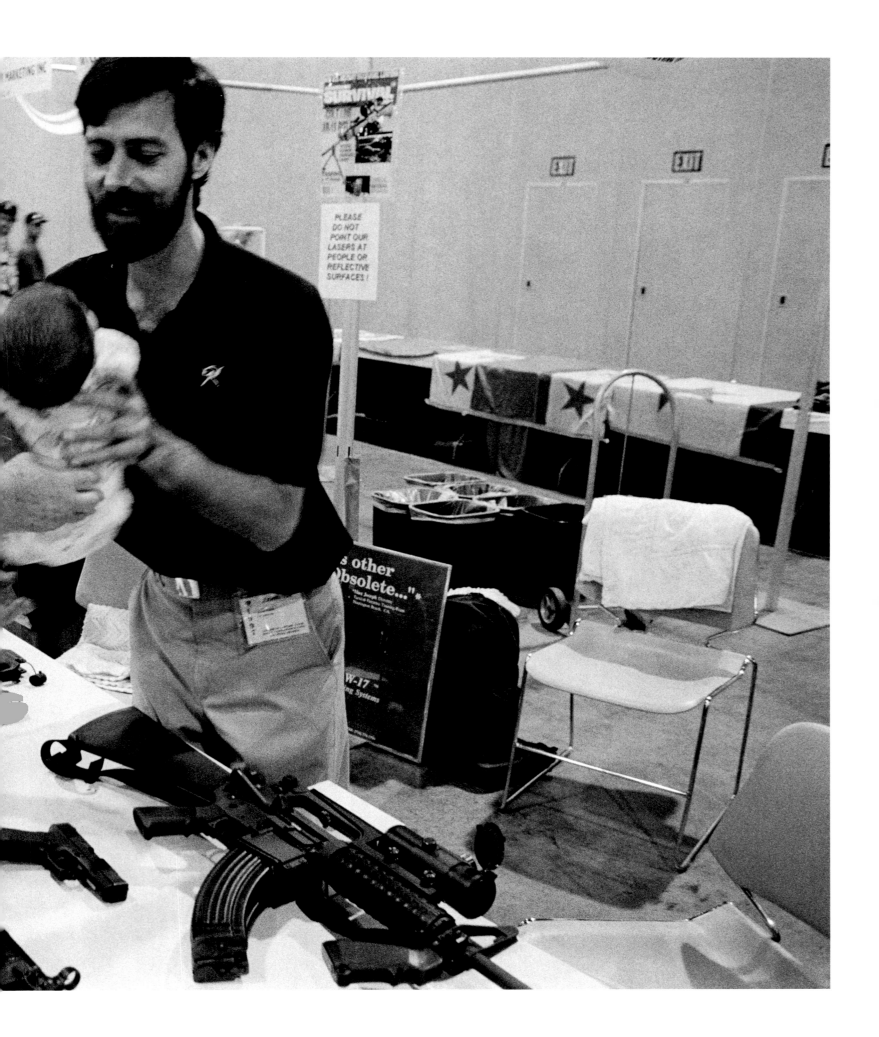

Funeral of gun-shot victim Joseph Chamberlin, Jr, 45.
Killed in the crossfire of an argument. New Hope Baptist Church, Memphis, Tennessee.

I'll never forget when we were on stake-out over in the projects. About six or seven dudes walked across in front of us and they each had a gun in their hand. We saw Mac-10's, pistols, shotguns, semi-automatic assault rifles…

OFFICER RICK CAMPBELL, DALLAS POLICE.

When I was undercover on narcotics I found out how they get their guns: the main dealer, if he has a clean record, he'll buy maybe 5-6 guns: 9mm auto's, Mac-10 machine-gun pistol 'street-sweepers', shotguns with 20-round canisters – it's unbelievable what you see out there on the streets. If the dealer can't buy them legally, if he hasn't got a clean record, they're bought legally by the drug dealers girlfriend, sister or brother, or just stolen from legal owners.

LTNT. DON ALDRIDGE, 45. OFFICER FOR 24 YEARS.

National Rifle Association 125th annual convention.

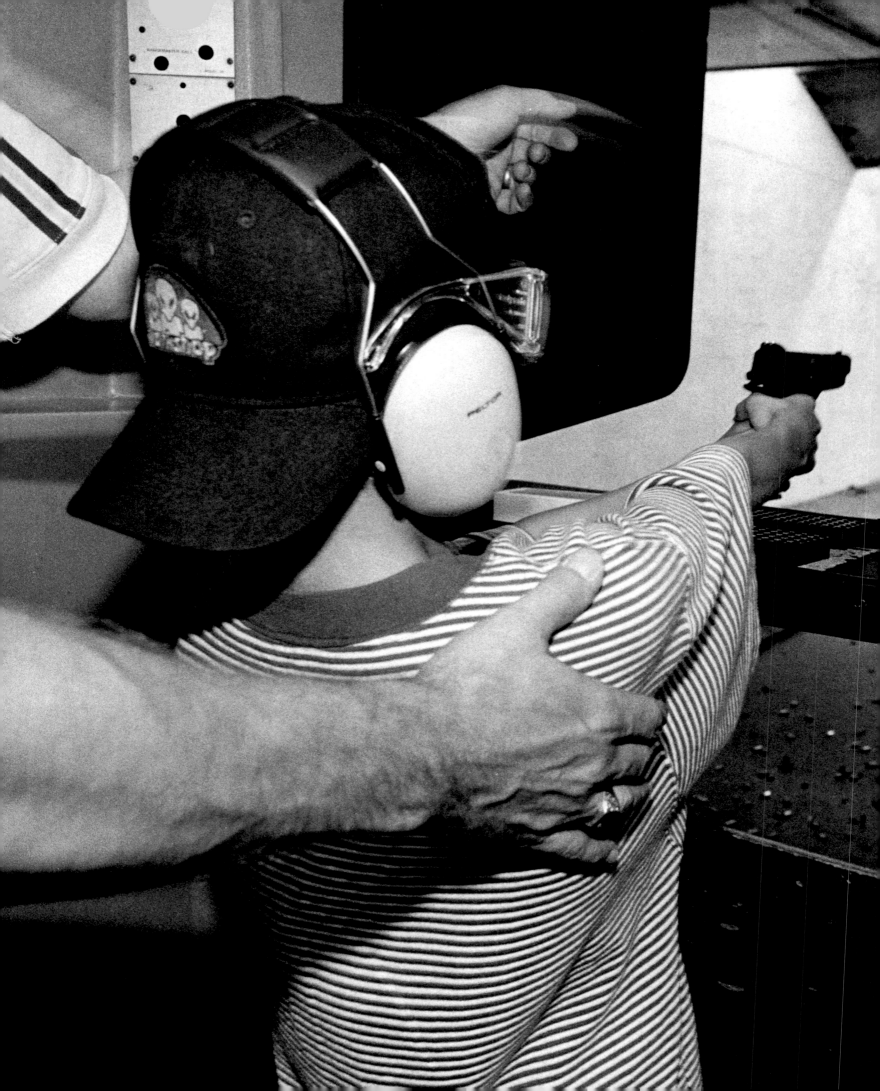

Smith & Wesson .44 magnum. Actual size.

THE GUN USED BY CLINT EASTWOOD'S MAVERICK COP 'HARRY', IN THE MOVIE *DIRTY HARRY.*

Guns and the right to bear arms is part of the fabric that makes America America, and you cannot remove that. If we were to turn the clock back and really look at how all these nations were formed, everybody had an axe and a sword and a rock. I think that's an equaliser: you've got a big stick and I've got a big stick – I'm not going to bother you…

UNIDENTIFIED POLICE OFFICER.

Part of the problem is stereotyping. The average American thinks that there are gang and drug wars and the people who get shot deserve it. But today, even the strongest advocates for guns have got to be sitting there thinking in the back of their mind, 'Jeez, look what happened! Is this gun stuff really rational?'.
Dr Ernest Moore, Chief of Surgery, Denver Health Medical Center.

Fifteen wooden crosses were anonymously erected on a hill overlooking Columbine High School, in memory of the twelve high school students and their teacher who were shot to death, and also the two student gunmen who ended their rampage by shooting themselves. A CROSS CONTROVERSIALLY ERECTED IN THE NAME OF DYLAN KLEBOLD, ONE OF THE TEENAGE KILLERS.

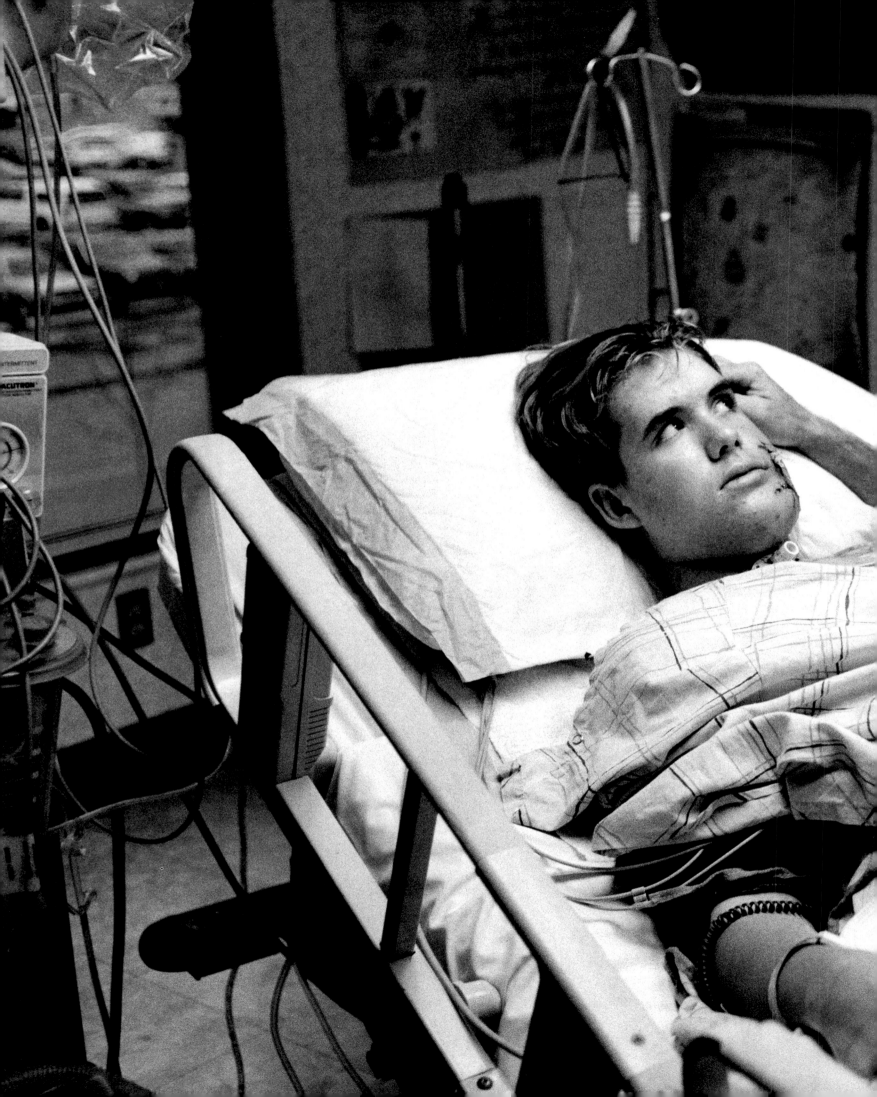

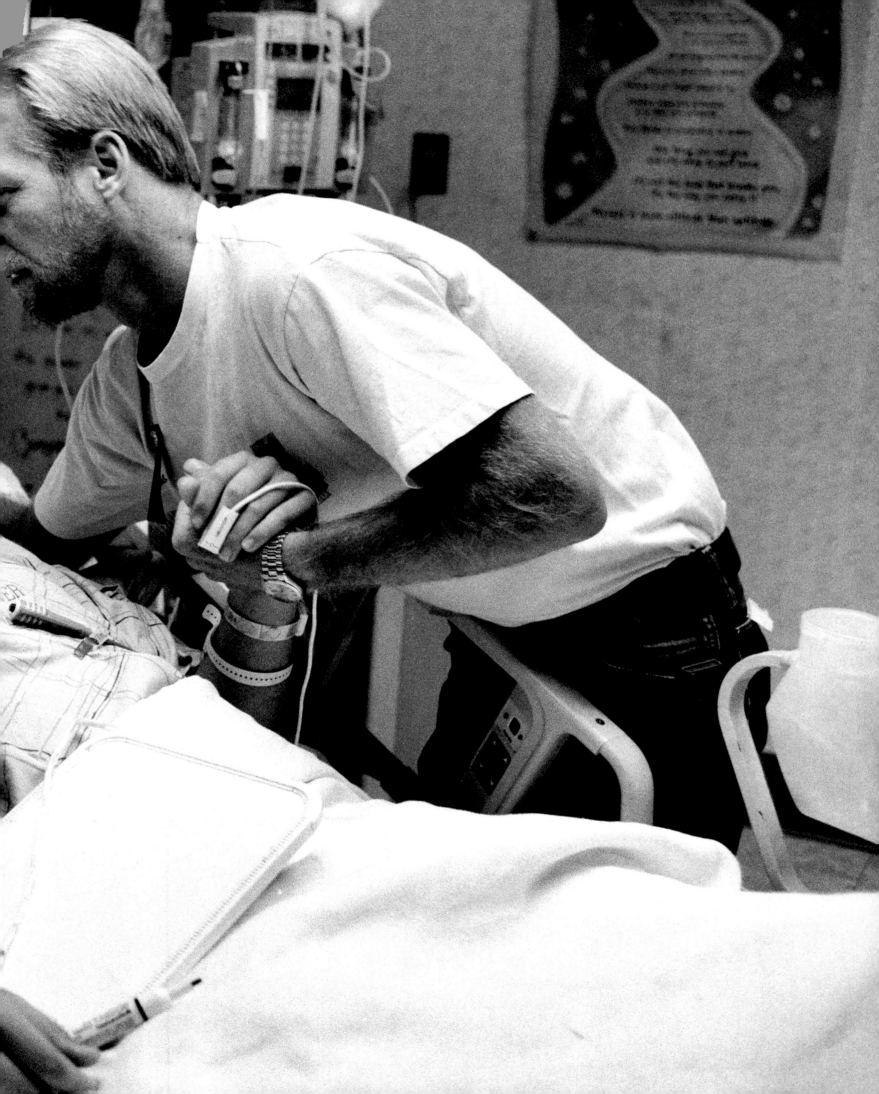

Lance Kirkland was shot in the chest, groin, legs and foot, by two school-mates carrying three different weapons. The teenage gunmen then shot him in the face at point-blank range with a sawn-off shotgun, leaving him for dead.

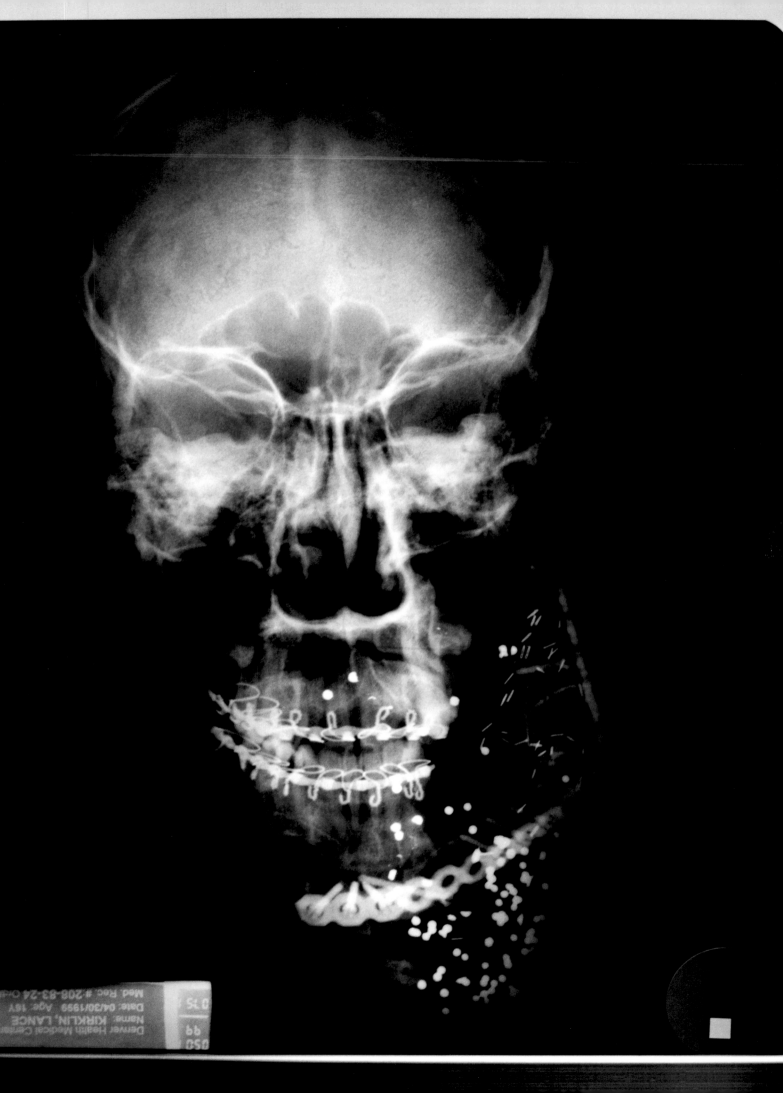

Tom Mauser, whose son was shot to death in the
Columbine High School rampage, addresses an
8,000-strong crowd on the steps of Denver State
Capitol building. The protest condemned the timing
of the NRA's annual meeting in Denver, ten days
after the local school shooting massacre.

Charlton Heston, President of the National Rifle Association (NRA), addresses a crowd of 2,000 pro-gun members at the Adam's Mark Hotel, while outside, 8,000 demonstrators protest the timing of the NRA's annual meeting in Denver in the aftermath of Columbine. Heston, responding to calls for tighter gun controls in the wake of the school shooting rampage, countered: 'In the words of Ben Franklin: "Those who would give up their freedom to purchase a little security… deserve neither freedom nor security".'

It would be fashionable to change my beliefs on gun ownership and the Second Amendment because of those children's deaths, but it's a matter of personal freedom...

Colorado gun-owner Lisa Boshard with her AR-15 semi-automatic assault rifle, used for 'recreational shooting and home defence'.

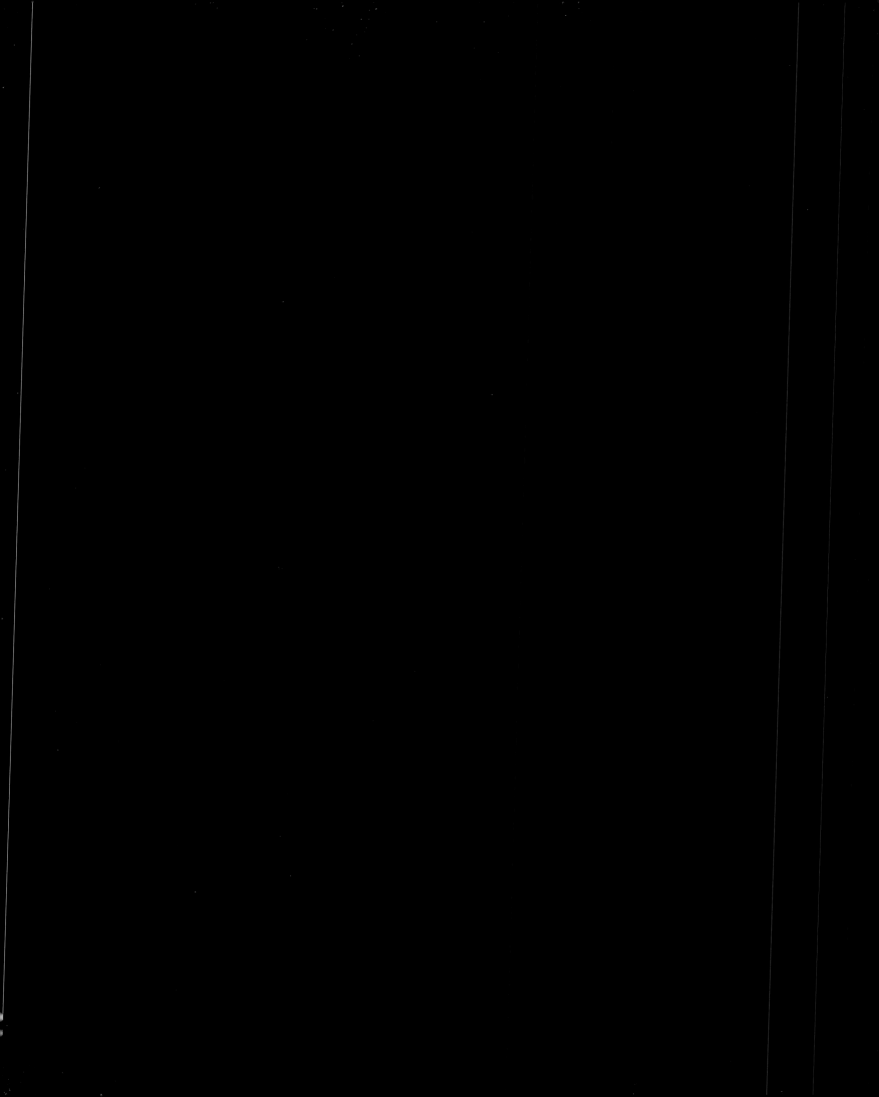

There is something profoundly distasteful about debating gun policy, from either side of the Second Amendment divide, in the context of the shock and mourning following such a tragedy.

Editorial in the Denver Rocky Mountain News, commenting on Bill Clinton's attempts to tighten gun-control laws, ten days after two high school students carried four locally-purchased firearms – including a semi-automatic assault-pistol loaded with 32-bullet magazines – into their school and opened fire on classmates, killing twelve students and a teacher, and hospitalising twenty-two others.

US Attorney General Janet Reno visits Littleton, Colorado
following the Columbine High School shooting spree.

Vice President Al Gore arrives in Littleton, Colorado, to attend
a public memorial service held in a shopping mall parking
lot, close to cordoned-off Columbine High School, the site of
the worst school shooting massacre in American history.

We try and do the best job we can. Sure, you may make one sale and that individual may do something bad with that weapon, and that's unfortunate and that's one of the drawbacks of being in the business. You do the best you can, you act as responsibly as you can, and that's really all you can do.

OWNER OF COLORADO GUNSTORE, ONE WEEK AFTER THE COLUMBINE SCHOOL MASSACRE.

In the days after the Columbine High School
shooting rampage, school districts around
the country banned trench coats and
considered uniforms to prevent pupils from
smuggling weapons and to break up cliques.
In the Western Massachusetts community of
Pitsfield, the City Council narrowly defeated
a bill to prohibit 'flamboyant and excessively
morbid dress' following the school massacre.
The Columbine teenage killers were reported
to have worn long dark coats to school.

PRAY FOR HEALING

In the days following the Columbine High School massacre, the vehicles of murdered students became shrines to their owners, visited by relatives and friends. JON TOMLIN VISITS HIS SON'S CHEVROLET IN THE GROUNDS OF THE SCHOOL.

The idea that anyone could freak out with a gun is certainly one motivation to own a gun. JASON HORN, 25, PURCHASES A HANDGUN ONE WEEK AFTER THE LOCAL COLUMBINE HIGH SCHOOL MASSACRE.

OVER 30,000 US CIVILIANS ARE KILLED BY GUNFIRE EVERY YEAR.

Afterword
Zed Nelson

I AM TOLD THERE ARE 240 MILLION GUNS IN THE UNITED STATES,

and that the number is increasing by some 5 to 7 million a year. They say that 90 people are shot dead every day, that over half a million people have been shot to death in the United States since 1960.

Other people say that there's no link between the availability of firearms and the annual death toll, that a gun is a tool, that people have always killed each other, and if they didn't use a gun, they'd use a rock, or a knife, or a stick.

A group of armed Memphis housewives warned "If you ban guns, the bad guys will still have them"; and a father holding a gun in one hand and his baby girl in the other voiced a widely held belief when he said "it's my constitutional right to own a hand gun, to protect myself and my family".

Who would argue against such basic sentiments? But who also can ignore the facts: The 'bad' guys tend to steal their guns from the 'good' guys, (or just buy them second hand without a background check), and protecting a family is hard when teenagers can legally purchase semi-automatic weapons through classified ads and at local gun shows across America.

THE PEOPLE WHO LIKE GUNS HATE THE PEOPLE WHO DON'T LIKE GUNS.

And the people who don't like guns hate the people who like guns. The gun manufacturers don't like the people who hate guns, but they like the people who like guns, and the politicians just want to be liked, so they may like or dislike guns, it depends who's asking.

California has banned assault weapons. But California is a great place to buy assault weapons nevertheless. Only they're not called assault weapons anymore. They're assault-style weapons. They have been given new technical names and cosmetically modified, so they're legal again. And the ones that are really banned, the ones with the old name-tag, they're still legal second-hand anyway.

At every new school shooting rampage or public shooting spree, somebody always seems to say, 'We thought we were in the safest place in America'. Each new atrocity appears to take place in a whiter, more suburban town than the last, inhabited by people who 'never thought it could happen here'.

IT'S A FUNNY THING THE GUN-DEBATE, BECAUSE THERE REALLY ISN'T MUCH OF A DEBATE.

You're either for, or against. And if you're rational, logical, and willing to compromise, you're out there in no-man's land, a traitor to both sides.

Acknowledgements
John Easterby for close involvement with
development, inspiration and editing, and Tara and
IPG agency, London, for their long-term commitment
to Gun Nation.

James Brown and Tony Chambers at *GQ* Magazine
for first publishing the story with flair and imagination.

Vikki Morgan for generously overseeing and helping
shape the book.

Richard Bull and Chris Thomson at Yacht and Gavin
Pretor-Pinney at the *Idler* for generously donating
their time and skills in the early stages of the book.

Simon Elliott at Rose Design for a brilliantly executed
book design.

Sophie Hicks at Ed Victor Ltd., for her enthusiasm
and commitment as book agent.

Gigi Giannuzzi, Nicholas Kenney and Mark Reynolds
for publishing Gun Nation in the spirit it required.

Herb Cook-Mack for research.

Andy Whitfield for assistance and support on the first
Gun Nation trip to the US.

Steve McCloud at Metro for printing the final images,
and Glen Brent for printing work in progress.

Daniel Lazare for an unforgettable introduction.

N BROKE

FOR FINGER

YO
BU

KID

THE SE

YOUR HONOR
ENTS ASS!

GUN-500

ONKING
OADING

Guns D
Peop